God made the ocean, but the Dutch made Holland.

~ Dutch Proverb

Don't make use of another's mouth unless it has been leant to you.

~ Belgian Proverb

When good Americans die they go to Paris.

~ Oscar Wilde

We Put Things In Our Mouths

the poet's experiences in Amsterdam, Brussels, Brugge and Paris

Rick Lupert

We Put Things In Our Mouths

Ain't Got No Press

Cover Photo, Design, and Layout ~ Rick Lupert
Author Photo ~ Addie Lupert

Thank you Addie, Hennie, Anne, René, Hans, Rembrandt, Salvador, Claude, The Pis Family, The Dutch, The Belgians, The French, the swans, and Brendan and Jayne who insisted we go to Belgium.

(818) 904-1021

or

15522 Stagg Street
Van Nuys, CA 91406

or

Rick@PoetrySuperHighway.com

or

PoetrySuperHighway.com

First Edition ~ January, 2010

ISBN: 978-0-9820584-1-1 $12.00

To Addie, the muse, the source of all poetry

DEPART   **DEPAR**

Trains au départ   Departur

Zeit Time Heure	Nach Destination Destination
11ʰ52	BRUXELLES-MIDI LIEGE AACHEN KOLN
11ʰ55	LILLE FLANDRES ROUBAIX TOURCOING
12ʰ04	PONT COMPIEGNE TERGNIER SAINT-QUE
12ʰ16	LONDON-WATERLOO
12ʰ19	ARRAS LENS BETHUNE HAZEBROUCK DUN
12ʰ22	PERSAN-BT CHAMBLY BORNEL MERU BEA
12ʰ28	CREIL LONGUEAU AMIENS
12ʰ52	BRUXELLES LIEGE AACHEN KOLN
12ʰ52	BRUXELLES BERCHEM ROTTERDAM AMSTE
12ʰ55	LILLE FLANDRES
2ʰ58	CALAIS FRETHUN ASHFORD LONDON-WAT
3ʰ22	PERSAN-BT CHAMBLY BORNEL MERU BEA
3ʰ26	CREPY VILLERS SOISSONS ANIZY-PINC
4ʰ07	CHANTILLY CREIL PONT COMPIEGNE TE
4ʰ16	LONGUEAU AMIENS ABBEVILLE ETAPLES
4ʰ22	BRUXELLES-MIDI
4ʰ25	LILLE FLANDRES
ʰ37	COMPIEGNE SAINT-QUENTIN AULNOYE
ʰ40	ASHFORD LONDON-WATERLOO
ʰ48	DAMMARTIN CREPY SOISSONS ANIZY L

NOUS VOUS RAPPELONS QUE L ENSEMBLE DE VOS BAGAGES

on the way

At Passport Control in Paris

With a baby
you can breeze to the front of the line
so the woman thinks
and no-one tells her "non"
So she is gone
and we are left
smelling each other

haiku

every time we leave
the house, even to the store
it's a honeymoon

haiku

in Paris we shared
a secret that won't appear
in my poetry

Amsterdam

In the Van Gough Museum

I want to take a photograph
of the woman who keeps saying
"no photography" and then I want to ask
her "oh yeah, what if I have
a photographic memory?"

In the Rijks Museum

I see a musket with testicles
it seems to make sense

At the Painting "Still Life With Turkey Pie" by Pieter Claesz

a found haiku with an extra six syllable line bonus

The viewers gaze is
immediately drawn to
the imposing pie

Crowned with a dead turkey

Not the Stairs

of course Addie
wants to go in
the giant glass
elevator

Places I Might Die

a glass elevator
a window seat on an airplane
in a puddle
Belgium

It's not that I want to die
in any of these places
or anywhere really

These are just
possibilities

On Prinsengracht

I

Roughly half a block
north of the Anne Frank House
sits a restaurant called
the Pancake Bakery
Thankfully, they do not serve
Anne Frankakes

II

Much to the chagrin of my ancestors
I cannot decide if Annecake
or Anne Frankake
is more funny

After a Healthy Meal in the Jordaan

Addie says "I'm going to burst."
I pause because I want to say just the right thing.

"I look forward to loving your guts"
falls out of my mouth

like a brick falling out of the mouth
of someone who had a brick in their mouth.

"Don't you love them already" she asks.
"Yes, but I mean physically" I say, having

constructed a new canal house out of
the materials which have excreted through my lips.

I had a little Micky Pet

says Addie upon returning from the bathroom
fortunately I knew the name of the restaurant's cat
was Micky, and there was no incident of molestation
by a certain famous Hollywood mouse.

In the Bathroom at the Rijks Museum

I create my own masterpiece.
Ahh...another city, another toilet

The Sentiment of the Previous Poem as a Haiku

In the bathroom at
The Rijks Museum I make
my own masterpiece

That Would be Too Many Cats at Once

"I want every cat in the world
to come to me right now
so I can pet them" I say
after I spot a second
inaccessible one through a window.
"That doesn't sound like a good idea"
says Addie "You might want to rethink that"
and, of course, she is right.

Haiku

That secret I wrote
about earlier, I'm still
not going to tell

Waking up Early in the City of Tolerance

I find six or seven AM
has me upright listening

to the local canal ducks arguing with
the neighborhood poodle.

I can hear the fig tree
getting taller in the garden.

Speaking of taller
a nice boy from Canada

named after a southern vegetable
reached up the side of the building

and picked grapes growing
on the neighbors vine.

I wonder if our plants in Van Nuys
have enough water

Hours go by and soon I'm thinking
nine AM sounds reasonable.

I will get wet from head to toe
eat a typical Dutch Breakfast,

then walk out the door to see what this
Venice of the North has to offer.

In the Jewish Historic Museum

There is a special exhibit of Sarah Bernhardt,
the greatest actress of her day

She had a Jewish mother
but that was about it.

They say she slept in a coffin and, after
an amputation, she performed with one leg.

They say she was so adept at dying on stage
that death scenes became mandatory

in all her films and plays. They say she never
died the same way twice. Her actual death

in 1923 may have been a disappointment.
There was a parade in Paris which

they called a funeral procession. They took her to
Père Lechaise. They say she died while

making a film. (They say) she
sleeps in a coffin now.

Poor Rembrandt

and I mean that literally
he couldn't pay his mortgage

and lost his house in the neighborhood
which took his name

Now one of the sponsors of the house
is the bank that holds our mortgage

Poor Rembrandt
I want to put him up in our Van Nuys guest room

Let him do realists of the ants and palms
I could talk to the bank, get him his house back

I'd put my signature on the papers
for him

Because of the Rain

Addie and I
huddle under a
closed pancake house
awning.

Our host told us
not to bring
an umbrella
it would just be a sprinkle.

No.
It is not a sprinkle. Our
dreams of pancakes
float away.

Sacred Cow

We are on a bus to the outskirts
to see windmills and the birth of cheese.

The tour guide repeats her speeches
in English, Italian and Spanish,
but I suspect it's not equal as
I recognize words in the other languages
I did not hear in mine.

I hear the word hamburger in Italian
and can only assume they are aware
we are American vegetarians
and will soon attack us with meat.

We are on guard.

Historicalism

Despite the water
retention properties of
freshly cut wooden shoes
wooden diapers
never caught on

I Can Feel My Sideburns are Different Lengths

Perhaps that's why none of the Italians on the bus
    are speaking to me.
It's possible that varying sideburn lengths
    are a great insult in Italian culture.
I've never heard of it, but, as I said,
    it's possible.

Everyone Takes Pictures of the Cheese Making Lady

she knows when to smile
she is the rock star of Gouda

Giant Wooden Shoe Couple

It is a requirement at all
wooden shoe factories to
have a giant wooden shoe outside.

Everyone already took pictures
in the giant wooden shoe at the first stop.
The giant shoe here sits lonely and unphotographed

Maybe this second giant wooden shoe
is married to the first one and they just
work in different places.

Nothing Makes Me Happier Than Free Cheese

That is to say excepting my wife
and maybe large sums of money
and good health
and all the cats in the world.

But besides that
here on the cheese farm
with the abundant free samples
I am very happy.

In Volendaam

Coca-Cola is delivered by truck
and then cart and then the hands of man
carry the cases into the restaurants.
Still, you are not able to carry the glass bottles away
in your hands for reasons no-one can explain.

Still In Volendaam

You can get cheap and fast seafood
but if you're a vegetarian or
you want to carry away a glass bottle
of Coke, you're pretty much screwed.

Marken - A History Lesson

I am on an Island in
the middle of the IJsselmeer Sea*
So you can imagine.

* It's just a lake now.

Romy Schneider in the Film Museum

We see our second dead actress
Romy Schneider, who died
beautiful at forty three.
Too young; but first her
husband's suicide, says the
woman collecting the tickets,
and then her son killed by a fence.
It was too much
and then one night of drugs and alcohol
were too much
and she was gone.
Three decades on the screen.
Actually she was our third dead actress
if you count Marilyn
in the sex museum.

Everything in Amsterdam is Under Construction

The unnatural beauty of the city
concealed by cranes and scaffolding.
The Royal Palace closed until another year.
The Rijks museum collection moved to a small
wing and a nearby church.
It was like this in 1996 in Paris.
My first time in these cities
where too much revealed at once
is, apparently, against my religion.

Oh Amsterdam

City of tolerance and soup
canals and pancakes
Your trams in their grooves
your red lights, your whores,

Oh Amsterdam,
there is a market on your corner
an art in your window
You, who turned in Anne Frank

your homo-monument.
Oh Amsterdam
The beer, the hash, the tulip
the wood shop

Half your people are syrup sweet
the other half mustard annoyed
Oh Amsterdam, I Amsterdam
The other vowels too Amsterdam

We think we like you
your dike, your pea soup
but we're not sure how you feel
about us.

Three Not Ideal Haiku With Explanations

I

> Amsterdam is be-
> low sea level. But don't look
> for fish in the streets

(These are the words I wanted to use but, awkwardly, to fit the haiku form it was necessary to split the word "below" between the first two lines. I call this technique 'embarrassing stupidity.")

II

> Amsterdam is well
> below sea level. Don't look
> for fish in the streets

(Here's an honest attempt at working the words and syllables into the proper haiku specifications. Unfortunately using the word "well" before "below sea level" could imply that the city is indeed much further below sea level than it actually is, taking emphasis away from the more important surreality of the lack of fish in the streets. Bring your submarine, this haiku seems to imply, when, in fact, flippers and a snorkel would do just fine.)

III

Thanks to dikes we are
below sea level. Don't look
for fish in the streets.

(Replacing the phrase "Amsterdam is" with "Thanks to dikes, we are" allows for a smoother flow into the haiku form. Especially pleasing is the opportunity to remove the filler word "but", giving a more pleasing minimalistic transition between the two sentences. However, "Thanks to dikes" also explains that there wouldn't be water in the streets anyway, which destroys the main "look for fish" thrust in the below sea-level world. Like a disassembled Lego space ship from years ago, sitting in a box and eventually set on fire.)

I Amsterdam

I
am not
Amsterdam

To Anne Frank

We slept in your neighborhood
visited your house where

a woman from the past
told us she last saw you

over a fence when you told her
you had no-one and so

she brought you food which
another woman stole and so

she brought you more food
threw it over the fence

and you caught it before the thieves
and she didn't see you again

You became one of many
too many

Not Free Transportation

We could have stolen
this train ride to Brussels
No-one checked our tickets

The closest thing was when
an Asian woman sat on Addie
As usual, she went with the flow.

Brussels

The Pis Family

Tonight in Brussels
so hungry we have two dinners
at same restaurant.

Confuses waitress who asks
"didn't you already eat?" we think,
it was French so could have been anything.

Two meals later we
drink Belgian beer next door.
I bump head on giant wheel,

walk away to see family of
pissing statues
and their dog.

French Class Was So Many Years Ago

I confuse the French word for half
and order a pizza with half cheese
and olives at noon

The Gospel of Jesus According to Addie

Jesus was a baby
Then he was crucified

This has been the gospel of Jesus
according to Addie.

Evolution According to Rick

I start to tell Addie
that mermaids evolved into
two legged mermaids which
evolved into monkeys which
eventually became people.
She stopped listening around
the time I said the word
mermaids.

The Musées royaux des Beaux-Arts de Belgique is the Anti-Louvre

At the Louvre
there are ninety-seven paintings
on every wall.

At the Musées royaux des Beaux-Arts de Belgique,
There are many walls with
no paintings at all

She Doesn't See War

Upon encountering a painting
where smoke billows above ships at sea
destroyed by cannon fire, Addie says
"Boat Clouds"

Upon Seeing a Painting Depicting
the Medieval Town of Anvers, France

I remark that this
is one of the many places I was born

and then decide this is one of the funniest comments ever made
in the history of oral communication.

Addie moves on to the next painting
so I can revel privately.

Satyr

We see a figure with a tail and goat legs.
"It's one of those half whatevers" Addie says.
We laugh until the cows in the next painting
come into view.

In Magritte's House

They make us put plastic socks over our shoes
before walking up the stairs.

"It protects the floors" the guide tells us
"But it's kind of surreal on it's own"
she adds with a wild-eyed smile.

Magritte Painted Half of His Work in This House

I tell Addie I like being in places where things happened.
She tells me things happen in most places where I am
which either completely disassembles my surrealist fantasy
or makes the mundane spectacular, as I stare at every brick
on the way back to the center of town.

We Drink Beer Below the Fifth Largest Church in Europe

The book tells us it is also the "most ghastly".
The waiter tries to upsell us with a plate of cheeses

but this is only a stop on the way to dinner,
so we decline. He seems disappointed

as buses go by and almost a car accident.
We wanted a plate of famous Belgian Frites but

he said it was not possible. Perhaps because they are
only for the locals or who knows what..

Time goes by. Addie works on her nails.
She is patient like a Trappist beer.

We have so much left to put in our mouths.
I am exhausted thinking about it.

At Friteland

I

We have entered several countries
but none have excited Addie more
than our arrival at Friteland.

II

At Friteland
I eat the fries
move closer to my
eventual heart attack
and watch the Wiener Bus go by

At Cantillon Brewery

At eleven o'clock in the morning
Brussels was made for beer.

The lambic samples we guzzle
took three years to make.

We tour the factory and
see the machines.

The young beer bottles, as big as champagne
stacked horizontally, ferment

before our eyes. The Brewery cat
follows us from room to room,

attacks when we let our guard down.
We watch the yeast eat the sugar.

We leave with the taste of raspberries
on our tongues.

A Day of Chocolate

"Don't buy chocolate from the Chinese" says the hotel man at breakfast and with that we are off for a day of chocolate and beer and every last-minute typical Belgian fare we can ingest.

In our first chocolate shop they greet us with "would you like a free sample" and how could one say no to such a thing. It is then we realize, on this street with chocolate shop after chocolate shop, that free samples offer an entire day's worth of activity. Soon the chocolate on our lips has the shops closing their doors as we approach.

We move on to beer, which we had for breakfast. We go in to the famous brand Belgian chocolate shop because why not check out the best. This chocolatier is so famous, they don't need to offer free samples, and they don't. A few minutes in to the store and two Chinese walk out of the back room. We remember the hoteliers words "It's not because they are Chinese, it's just not authentic." and we are back on the street faster than you can say Free Tibet.

Another chocolateuse is lonely and she speaks with us about Los Angeles and the Atlantic coast of France. She has large eyes as blue as the walls in Magritte's living room. She tells us to go to the other shops for better quality. It's only a temporary job until she returns to France. Her big eyes are blue like the sky Magritte painted.

On the Train to Brugge

The Grim Reaper and his wife sit across from us
on the train to Brugge.

Ahh so this is how it ends, I think
as outside the window, Belgian cows take the day off.

The reapers have eyes like death
or, if you prefer, a pale horse.

Missus reaper gets up to use the bathroom
and then they both exit the train at Aalter

More of Belgium rolls by and we are elated.
We will live to see Paris

Brugge

Scheme Inspired by Knowledge

Today I learn a triptych
is a three-paneled painting
and not just a travel guide
given for free by the Auto Club

Perhaps I can confuse
the people at my local triple A
and get them to give me
a priceless Hans Memling.

This Was Written In My Journal and I Have No Idea What It Means

I F I R9 ot GM I B

The Assault

Man, could Magritte paint nipples.
A slaughtered ball.

The Judgement of Cambyses
(Gerard David, 1498)

I see a painting in which a man is flayed alive
meaning his skin is removed from his body.
Now that I know what flayed means, I can be sure
to not accidentally request it.

Alert, Alert, Beer is Coming

is what our taste buds say as they watch the froth disappear
according to the beer woman at the Brugge brewery

"You are to converse with the beer until the head is gone"
she continues. "If it speaks back, it is time to go home."

Make Your Own Kind of Music

At the fish market built by Napoleon
I stand in one of the stone stalls and shout

"Fish! Fish!" into the square.
It does not help that I have no fish.

Again my wife disappears
into Belgian anonymity.

A Sculpture

Addie sees a man inside a banana.
I tell her it is a man inside the moon.
There is much laughter.

At de Bier Temple - My Heart Is In The East

At the shop called Beer Temple
I try to organize a minyan

It is impossible because there aren't enough
people and the shop faces north.

Anyway, the store owner is
more concerned with selling beer

than the direction of Jerusalem.

The Swans are Organizing

At night we see two swans
wading away from the main swan area
towards, perhaps, the North Sea.

They meet up with
two more at a canal intersection
and then two more a little further.

The swans have not organized
like this since the revolution.
Things are afoot.

Because Flemish Food is Chiefly Dead

We eat across Africa.
Morocco, Ethiopia and South Africa.

No matter how you slice it
Rabbit is not vegetarian.

Leaving Brugge

Brugge, your wet cobblestones,
your three hundred and sixty steps up.

Your bells ringing in our ears.
We watch your horses stand on two feet.

We dance with your Flemish Elvis.
An old hospital which heals only paintings now.

You tell us the story of beer and chocolate
in three languages. Our tongue waits it's turn.

Finally the train away. Thank you Belgium.
Thank you Magritte and Memling.

Monet,
we are on our way to you.

Frugal at the Train Station

I spend a lengthy period of time
in the train station bathroom because
it costs fifty cents to get in and
I want to get my money's worth.

Continuing to Make My Own Kind of Music

I yell "Fish!" one last time
in the train station, still without
fish, and still with my wife
disavowing all knowledge.

Thinking of Paris

If I were Jacques Prévert
Ahh hell I've got nothing
I'm not Jacques Prévert

Paris

Première Nuit à Paris

We take the Metro to Montmartre,
our first view of the city.

Concerned the Eiffel Tower has been removed
for the summer. Relieved to find it behind a tree.

Walk past Sacré-Couer. Plan on taking left but
a witch with broom, a man with giant nose and

five other oddly costumed Frenchies
walk dramatically by

Realize imperative to follow them
So we go right into Place du Tertre

They walk around square disrupting diners
until unrelated man chases them away with giant toothbrush.

Thanks to this diversion, we find restaurant with tofu.
I'm not making any of this up.

Our first night in Paris.

"If I could live anywhere besides Los Angeles, it would be here"

is a sentence I've said
everywhere I've visited.
But this is Paris, so
it counts double.

Petit Déjeuner

We awake to
Brazilian coffee.

We lick our cups,
as we are known to do.

The croissant is larger
than Addie's head.

Cold Toes Ahead

The weather forecast
and the hovering clouds

say it is not wise to
have one's toes exposed today.

But vacations are not a time for wisdom
especially in Paris.

We throw our passports
out the window

and head out the hotel door
for Monet's garden.

I thought I Might Die in Amsterdam

but after two sex museums, two
chocolate museums, three breweries
and a number of cardiovascular experiences
there hasn't been a single inappropriate palpitation.
We head to Montmartre to put fondue inside us.

The August Surprise

The last several days
I've written "July" in my journal
as if I could travel through time
with my pen.

French Things

The French tile
on our hotel toilet floor is nice.

It compliments the French door knob,
French wicker table and French duvet cover.

I'm particularly fond of the
French noises outside the window.

Musée des Canards

They have a museum
for almost everything here,
but not ducks.

The ducks probably
wouldn't stay on the pedestals
which would lead to frustration for everyone.

Our First Morning Without Having to Select a Breakfast Time

We become bad soldiers of the army of earliness.
I hear French people in the next room through
the bathroom wall. We will join forces and
accomplish nothing before noon.

Paris in the Rain

Let's just say
it's wetter.

At the Musée Rodin

The Thinker.
What's he thinking about?
Probably pants.

Auguste Rodin, 1840-1917

The old men of his time
saw the French Revolution.

He never knew
World War One.

Got the great Japanese actress (Hanako)
to take off her clothes.

The Beer Effect

One night a French boy emerges from the Latin Quarter and yells "PARIS" in my ear. He decides we are from America and welcomes us to France by shaking my hand with his, wet with alcohol.

Soon his friend arrives and apologizes. The first boy removes a full glass of beer from his coat and pours it over his face. Some goes in his mouth, the rest forms rivers down the front of his clothes. He thows the glass in any direction. It shatters in the middle of Place Saint-Michel.

We decide it is time to go and quickly head into the ground under a sign which reads "Metropolitan." The second boy says "No really, we are okay" as they follow us into the Metro where a new crowd of people distracts them and their howls.

Soon we are on a train thinking only of tomorrow.

Foot or Train

Although the hotel is walking distance
we decide to take the Metro because of the rain.
When discussing this decision, Addie says
"it would be better to not be 'out of the ground.'"
I, and the earthworms, agree.

Haiku

A grinding noise means
twenty euro discount and
free extra pillows

Conversation About How Addie's Toes are Still Black From Yesterday's Sandals, Even After Showering

Rick - "Maybe you're becoming a Negro."
Addie - "One toe at a time?"

Art Appreciation

It is hard work looking at art
noticing the details of a complex canvas

> *the seemingly out of place steam ship*
> *in the upper right hand corner*

Remembering these details when looking
at other paintings

Realizing the similarity
between the two pieces and

then trying to remember the dates
so you can imagine who influenced who

Seeing texture and no texture
Coming home to your own city where

you rarely look at art and
feeling guilty about that

> *The weight of that guilt*

Deciding to put a painting on your wall
so maybe you'll look at it

as you eat your artless breakfast
drive your artless car to your artless desk

If this is you
Maybe it is not

Your omelette
a sculpture

La Vasque Fleurie - Kees Van Dongen

The painting is called "The Flowery Vase"
and indeed there is one, but also

a nude woman looking into a mirror.
Her eyes looking at you in the mirror,

a pearl necklace around her neck,
a dog on the floor.

New Color

We discover a blue
which on its own
illuminates itself

despite any bright background
or nearby source of light.
This blue, on a man,
covering a canvas
as a blackboard
it makes gold out of oil

establishes a self powered cabaret
This blue,
No, wait, it's purple.

Diana Ross - Bernard Rancillac 1974

We see a painting labeled "Diana Ross."
"That's Diana Ross" Addie says.

"Those are actually French words which mean..."
and then she walks away from me before I can finish.

Some Museums

require multiple visits
to take it all in

and then there are some paintings
which require many viewings

over the course of your lifetime
before you can begin

We're Getting Somewhere

Addie wouldn't let me stand naked in the garden
and pretend to be a statue because
I didn't look bronze or plaster.

So I ask her again when I discover
an empty alcove at the Modern art Museum
where I think it would be more appropriate.

She says she supposes, as long as I
ask for permission first. I'm just glad
she's warming up to the idea.

At the Airport

Smart cars are smart
because they are small.
I see an even smaller car.
It must be brilliant.

About The Author

The author as Salvador Dali standing in René Magritte's courtyard in Brussels.

Rick Lupert has been involved in the Los Angeles poetry community since 1990. He served for two years as a co-director of the Valley Contemporary Poets, non-profit organization which produces readings and publications out of the San Fernando Valley. His poetry has appeared in numerous magazines and literary journals, including *The Los Angeles Times, Chiron Review, Zuzu's Petals, Caffeine Magazine, Blue Satellite* and others. He edited *A Poet's Haggadah: Passover through the Eyes of Poets* anthology and is the author of eleven other books: *Paris: It's The Cheese, I Am My Own Orange County, Mowing Fargo, I'm a Jew. Are You?, Feeding Holy Cats, Stolen Mummies, I'd Like to Bake Your Goods, A Man With No Teeth Serves Us Breakfast* (Ain't Got No Press), *Lizard King of the Laundromat, Brendan Constantine is My Kind of Town* (Inevitable Press) and *Up Liberty's Skirt* (Cassowary Press). He has hosted the long running Cobalt Café reading series in Canoga Park since 1994 and is regularly featured at venues throughout Southern California.

Rick created and maintains the Poetry Super Highway, a major internet resource for poets. (PoetrySuperHighway.com)

Currently Rick works as the music teacher and graphic and web designer for Temple Ahavat Shalom in Northridge, CA and for anyone who would like to help pay his mortgage.

Rick's Other Books

A Man With No Teeth Serves Us Breakfast
Ain't Got No Press ~ May, 2007

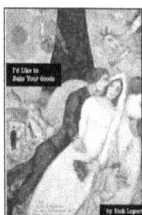

I'd Like to Bake Your Goods
Ain't Got No Press ~ January, 2006

STOLEN MUMMIES
Ain't Got No Press ~ February, 2003

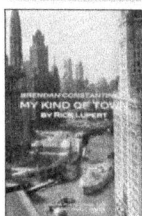

BRENDAN CONSTANTINE IS MY KIND OF TOWN
Inevitable Press ~ September, 2001

up liberty's skirt
Cassowary Press ~ March, 2001

FEEDING HOLY CATS
Cassowary Press ~ May, 2000

I'm a Jew, Are You?
Cassowary Press ~ May, 2000

MOWING FARGO
Sacred Beverage Press ~ December, 1998

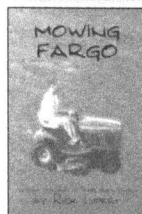

Lizard King of the Laundromat
The Inevitable Press ~ February, 1998

I Am My Own Orange County
Ain't Got No Press ~ May, 1997

Paris: It's The Cheese
Ain't Got No Press ~ May, 1996

For more information:
http://PoetrySuperHighway.com/

www.ingramcontent.com/pod-product-compliance
Lightning Source LLC
Chambersburg PA
CBHW062003040426
42447CB00010B/1888